James Douglas

Canadian Independence, Annexation and British Imperial Federation

James Douglas

Canadian Independence, Annexation and British Imperial Federation

ISBN/EAN: 9783337186593

Printed in Europe, USA, Canada, Australia, Japan

Cover: Foto ©ninafisch / pixelio.de

More available books at **www.hansebooks.com**

Canadian Independence

Annexation and

British Imperial Federation

BY

JAMES DOUGLAS

G. P. PUTNAM'S SONS
NEW YORK　　　　　　LONDON
27 West Twenty-third Street　　24 Bedford Street, Strand
The Knickerbocker Press
1894

COPYRIGHT, 1894
BY
JAMES DOUGLAS
Entered at Stationers' Hall, London
BY G. P. PUTNAM'S SONS

Electrotyped, Printed and Bound by
The Knickerbocker Press, New York
G. P. PUTNAM'S SONS

PREFACE.

The following essay is the amplification of an essay written for Canadian readers by a Canadian long resident in the United States.

Annexation implies a transaction to which the two sections concerned must be parties, and therefore is of importance, if not equally momentous, to both. To Americans the annexation, not alone of Canada, but of any further territory and its inhabitants, should be considered in the light of the perilous growth of sectionalism at home.

The problem of reconciling local interests and prejudices with the national well-being and will, is presenting itself obstinately for solution wherever representative government is on its trial, whether under its most restricted form or its most democratic development. By the Austrian Empire the German, Slavonic, and Magyar elements have to be conciliated. In Germany the Polish provinces, with their racial and religious divergences from the Teutonic mass of the people, have to be propitiated. In Great Britain the Irish question is the supreme puzzle to each succeeding administration, and keeps the legislative halls, if not the country, in a state bordering on revolution; while in the United States one must be blind not to recognize the existence of sectionalism, and as perversely obtuse to the threatening danger as men were before the war, not to be alarmed at the consequences of its growth. Why, therefore, add another story to the political structure? It is possible to make a constitutional edifice topheavy, and to crush the strongest foundation by piling on it more than the builders designed it to bear.

That the freest possible commercial intercourse and utmost political and social harmony should exist between the adjacent countries allied in so many ways, no one can question; but commercial engagements can be easily modified, close political ties are generally broken only amid rack and ruin. The customs tariffs now under discussion in this country and in Canada indicate an approach towards friendlier and more liberal international intercourse. The motion recently made in Congress in favor of international co-operation in opening up navigation between the great lakes and tidal waters points hopefully in the same direction.

Only the veriest optimist will assert that the complicated problems involved in representative government have been solved by any one of the self-governing communities of the world. If so, success will soonest be attained if the grand experiment be tried by many separate nations (provided each be large enough to make its results conclusive), rather than by huge aggregations of people, unwieldy by their numbers, and heterogeneous in their interests and habits.

It is significant that the present Prime Minister of England, chosen by the Liberal party, should be a Peer, a Radical, and a staunch Imperial Federalist, at one time President of the Imperial Federation League, and that Lord Rosebery supports Irish Home Rule, not as a piece of exceptional legislature, but as the first step towards the creation of a group of separate English-speaking states in both hemispheres, controlling without interference their own domestic affairs, but bound together by common constitutional ties and common interests, each working out its own individual destiny, while contributing to the strength, the influence, and the prosperity of the whole.

J. D.

NEW YORK, April 25, 1894.

CONTENTS.

CHAPTER	PAGE
I.—THE IMMINENCE OF POLITICAL CHANGE IN CANADA	1
II.—IMPERIAL FEDERATION POSSIBLE ONLY AS THE CONSEQUENCE OF INDEPENDENCE	11
III.—ANNEXATION AS AN ALTERNATIVE TO INDEPENDENCE	34
IV.—CANADA'S SLOW PROGRESS (COMPARED WITH THAT OF AUSTRALIA AND THE UNITED STATES) DUE TO PHYSICAL CONDITIONS	46
V.—IF THE "NATIONAL" OR PROTECTION POLICY HAS FAILED TO ATTRACT POPULATION TO CANADA, WILL ANNEXATION DO SO? . . .	55
VI.—PROBABLE EFFECT OF ANNEXATION ON CANADIAN INDUSTRIES AND WAGES.	65
VII.—ANNEXATION FROM THE STANDPOINT OF COMPARATIVE POLITICS . .	83
VIII.—ANNEXATION FROM AMERICAN AND CANADIAN POINTS OF VIEW . .	97
INDEX	111

CANADIAN INDEPENDENCE.

CHAPTER I.

THE IMMINENCE OF POLITICAL CHANGE IN CANADA.

The political future of Canada should and does occupy a foremost place in the thoughts of its people, and is a subject of no inconsiderable importance to her neighbor. It may be true that at present there is no widespread discontent with its existing constitution and relations, but some change in the alliance between Canada and the mother-country must, sooner or later, take place, as inevitably the relations between parent and child alter when childhood passes into boyhood and boyhood merges into manhood.

The parental-control stage of Canadian history ended in 1842. Since then Canada has been out of leading-strings, managing her own internal affairs, and trying to work out a system of government, based on representative principles, which would harmonize discordant elements at the centre, and permit of the absorption and development of territory at the periphery of her possible domain. The mother-country has held over her the ægis of her protection, which, happily, has never had to ward off a dart actually thrown. She has been ready to advise her offspring, to lend her money, and in every way assist her during this period of national adolescence. Now that this period has passed, it will be as ignominious to remain dependent and accept support from the parent state, as it is on the part of a full-grown man to look to his sire, not only for counsel, but for assistance.

A man is never too old to ask and take advice without derogation to his dignity, but he cannot accept alms without loss of self-esteem. He may enter a partuership penniless and yet contribute in energy and industry more in value than his partner's wealth. Into some such partnership the children of the great British family might be incorporated. Some such compact for mutual profit and protection there may arise a statesman endowed with the wisdom to frame and the sagacity and tact to manage. As yet, however, and though every thoughtful Englishman at home and in the colonies knows that to be the most momentous if not the most urgent question of the day, no feasible plan of Imperial Federation has been formulated. Meanwhile the impending crisis, which will be created out of some unforeseen complication, approaches.

In the case of the colonies in the Southern Hemisphere no outward pressure or internal convulsion threatens to create necessity for sudden decision and prompt action. As less and less territory remains to be occupied or seized in the Archipelago of the South Pacific by England or her rivals, the most pregnant cause for irritation there is disappearing. Australia's debt is by far the largest per capita of any community in the world. It is $230.78 per head, while the national debt per head of this country is only $14.24. As this enormous sum is due in greatest part to England, it serves as a balance-wheel to regulate the relations of the borrower and the lender, and tends to repress hasty action by the one or the other.

In South Africa a collision between the British and the Dutch or Portuguese communities might hasten disruption of existing relations, but it would probably have the opposite result, for the colonies acting in unison would be stronger than their antagonists; and political considerations would probably not restrain the parent state from tendering assistance should such a complication arise.

But on this continent a grave difference of policy between Canada and its neighbor may arise at any moment, on an economical question affecting, for instance, international commerce by land or water. Such a dispute might speedily lead to consequences which would produce distress on one side of the line and irritation on the other, and endanger good-fellowship and neighborliness. It is certain that the offence would have to be very clearly chargeable to the United States and would have to assume the gravity of an international affront, before England would embroil herself in a quarrel on account of Canada. In the event of reluctance on the part of England to champion Canada's cause, general discontent would ensue with the existing anomalous relations, which very reasonably deny Canada control of foreign affairs, though they expose her to all the consequences of a quarrel for which she may not be even remotely responsible.

Nevertheless every Canadian must in fairness admit that as long as Canada depends on England for defence against foreign foes, and neither supports an army and navy of her own, nor contributes to the maintenance of the Imperial forces, she should be denied the power of compromising the parent state by engaging in independent foreign negotiations.

Thus, while we can easily conceive of international complications arising which would create a crisis, Canada is at the same time certainly suffering from internal morbid conditions of the body politic, which will call, ere long, for the application of some remedy.

Nowhere in the British Empire are the external and internal incentives to change as imminent and threatening as here, and nowhere are the alternative policies which offer themselves more perplexing. No plan yet proposed meets with even wide approval, for none is free from grave objections.

The *far niente* policy would be the best if all Canada's internal forces should slumber; and all external foes, should she have any, would remain dormant. But, if she indulges in the hallucination that while the world revolves she can stand still, she will certainly find herself in the same sorry plight as the "foolish virgins," with no oil, no light, and no home. As a people Canadians should act with the same prudence and foresight that they bring to bear on their private affairs, make plans for their future guidance, whether Providence permits them to carry them out or not, and face the future manfully, determined that they will steer a straight course towards a definite goal, and try and shape their destiny in imitation of some worthy model.

Fortunately or unfortunately, circumstances do not point to any conspicuous goal as that towards which Canada should steer.

If we compare Canada's position with that occupied by the old colonies, and the prevalent sentiment of the Dominion with that which the colonists entertained towards the mother-country, we can conceive how much easier it was for them, once a break of existing relations occurred, to decide upon a course of action than it is for Canada. The Puritan immigrants were Englishmen, it is true, but they left their homes because their opinions and practices were at variance with those of the government and of the majority of their fellow-countrymen; and ever and anon, during the century and a half which intervened between the date of their landing on Plymouth Rock and the outbreak of hostilities, there were mutterings of the hurricane which was brewing.

At one time colonists resented the interference of Parliament because they belonged to a Crown colony. At another time they protested against the dictation of the Crown, because it trenched upon their liberties as Englishmen. One cannot read the story of the gathering of the storm without feeling that thunder and lightning were stored in that sultry atmosphere, and a tempest was liable at any moment to burst. Not only Samuel Adams, but many another colonist, had made up his mind before the crisis arose that a collision must occur and separation result. The opinions of some at least of the influential colonists were but the fruit of their wishes, and their wishes were the flames which kindled the revolution.

The case is different with Canada. The sentiment of the great bulk of the people is distinctly and strongly English. The large majority which the Conservative party commands is due primarily to a suspicion that, under the guise of commercial union with the United States, advocated by the Liberal party, are hidden designs for political union; and from this, which means a severance of those strong, sympathetic ties which bind English Canadians to the old country, the hearts of the majority of Canadians revolt. So long as England and Home are synonymous terms in Canadian speech, the sentimental bond attaching the child to the parent will be too strong to yield to merely economical considerations. Canadians have not and never have had a serious grievance against the parent country, for the disaffection of 1837 was far from being shared by the people at large, and it left hardly a trace of bitterness towards the mother-land. The legislative independence, which rewarded not only the rebels, but their foes, long ago obliterated any rancor excited by the event.

If, as one result of the almost absolute independence which ensued, the racial alienation between the Canadian French and the Canadian English is growing into racial antipathy, this antagonism is **traceable** to internal causes, and does not originate in animosity towards England. Thus, though there may be urgent reasons for changing Canada's constitution and modifying the terms of her alliance to the Empire, these reasons do not spring from discontent with the policy and action of the parent state, and consequently they do not, as in the case of the revolting colonists of last century, indicate the direction in which the change should be made.

CHAPTER II.

IMPERIAL FEDERATION POSSIBLE ONLY AS THE CONSEQUENCE OF INDEPENDENCE.

In reality there are but two alternatives open, either Annexation or Independence, more or less complete. A third course, that of Imperial Federation, if it be effected, is more likely to follow as a consequence of a scheme of independence than to precede it; for any feasible plan of Imperial Federation necessarily involves virtual independence of the federated States. Were the colonies still colonies, subject, even nominally, to interference by the central state, arguments coming from her would savor of commands, and suggestions of coercion. No people are so sensitive to slights as little people, and weak persons are most prone to stand on their dignity, as they have generally little else to stand upon.

The discussion of a scheme of British Imperial Federation, with a view to its actual realization, would lead to practical results, only if carried on between perfectly independent autonomous powers. The powers may differ widely in strength and resources, and thus differing, modify their claims in conformity with their real importance, but it almost follows without argument that it would be impossible to reconcile the divergent interests of the many branches of the British family, did not each enter the family council with the fullest rights of independent action.

Strong as may be its attachment to the parent state, every community would resent the faintest suspicion of pressure, and it is almost certain that were absolute independence of all the contracting parties not a precedent, pressure would almost inevitably follow reluctance on the part of any member of the proposed league to follow the policy which the majority might agree to. Consent wrung by pressure never becomes cordial acquiescence. Canada's Maritime Provinces, rightly or wrongly, believed themselves cajoled, if not coerced, into the confederation, and they have never entirely rid themselves of a certain sense of injury.

How independence is to be worked out, circumstances will probably indicate. It must not be effected by violent means. The genius of the English race favors the introduction of political and social changes, so great as to be revolutionary in their effects, by slow, constitutional means. But the changes must be seen and recognized to be necessary and salutary, and means must be put in motion to bring them about. Let independence become a distinct issue, not in party politics, but in the national aspirations and aims of all the great groups of the British family, and Independence will come about without clash of arms or severance of sympathetic ties.

Participation by right and not merely by courtesy, over its foreign, as well as its domestic affairs, must be exercised by every self-governing community. Dependence on themselves, and on their own diplomatic skill, as well as, when necessary, on their own strength, can alone build up a vigorous, self-reliant, national character in any people ; while, on the other hand, reliance on a foreign power, even though it be a parent state, enfeebles and degrades.

Great Britain has recognized in fact the rights of her colonies to participate in all deliberations with foreign powers, when their interests are affected ; but, as in the recent Behring Sea deliberations, the foreign power is naturally irritated, and the negotiations are embarrassed, by the fact that Canada could not make her side known by direct utterances of her own diplomatic agents, and that Great Britain had more than once to shift her position in deference to the wishes, secretly expressed, of her dependency. How far this was really the case or not, the United States public cannot, of course, know, but the suspicion of its being true did not raise Canada in the estimation of her neighbor, nor smooth the path of British diplomacy.

The Constitution of an Imperial Federation will have to be drawn on lines not heretofore laid down for any ship of state.

It is inconceivable, for instance, that such widely separated members of the British family as the Canadian, the Australian, the South African, and the West Indian groups, would yield so much of their sovereign rights to any Federal Government, as the States of the Union yield to the Government of the United States, which is not only theoretically, but actually and locally, an embodiment of themselves, nor would they delegate to their representatives to the Federal Parliament, sitting and deliberating at a distance from home and under the influence of the central powers, with its magical over-weening spell, derived from the prestige of age and parentage, the same control as the people of the Republic entrust to their representatives in Congress.

The impossibility of applying any system similar to the American Constitution, is indicated by the sense of incompatibility which influences the public mind of the people of the United States when the question of annexation of any distant territory is presented.

To do so seems like making a breach of

continuity and homogeneity, for the federated states are all geographically adjacent and all more or less peopled by men of single impulses and interests. So the tie which can bind, without irritating, such scattered communities as we have enumerated, must derive its strength from unanimity of national sentiment, from reverence for a common historical past, and a determination to maintain and live up to the political principles which underlie the self-government of all Anglo-Saxon communities, however diverse may be the form and fashion of the institutions through which they see fit to apply these principles. A common selfish interest may be the impelling motive, but it will really in the long run be a more feeble cohesive influence than the sympathetic.

If we glance back to that most instructive century and a half, between the landing of the Pilgrim Fathers, and the Declaration of Independence, we see how much more sensitive the colonies were to parliamentary than to kingly interference. They were willing to recognize a certain titular sovereignty as residing in the king, but resented any approach to parliamentary meddling. Had their charters conferred somewhat more ample power, and been religiously respected, and had the crisis not been precipitated by the gross stupidity and ignorance of English statesmen, and the perverse obstinacy of an English king, that deeply implanted reverence which all Englishmen feel for the king as the head of the state, and the representative of the people of all classes and all parties, supposed to be unswayed by political ambition, and holding the balance between opposing factions, might have been potent enough to restrain the allegiance of the colonies towards the parent state, till broader views of colonial independence had grown up, and a less officious king sat upon the throne.

Reasoning from the past, if the so-called dependencies of Great Britain are to continue to be affiliated to the old country, harmony will be maintained only if each is free to shape its own course in foreign as well as in domestic affairs, except where the wider interests of the whole are concerned. Each must in fact be a perfectly independent power, acting in concert, where the interests of trade and commerce and the momentous question of mutual defence demand, but bound to the mother-country and the other members of the family politic, not so much by rigid constitutional fetters as by the sympathetic ties of common blood, common aims, pride in a glorious past, and aspirations towards a still more glorious future.

But such a co-fraternity can be better effected and the institutions by which it is to be made operative and maintained can be better conceived and created, once the idea of dependence has been banished from the thoughts of Englishmen of both the Greater and the Lesser Britain, and the sense of *inter*-dependence in its highest meaning has permeated the conceptions of all the free independent people of English nationality. They may be widely separated geographically, and the forms of government may differ widely in details, but all must embody, and all must apply to their diversified conditions of industrial and social life, the same fundamental principles of liberty and self-government which Englishmen brought over to Jamestown and to Plymouth, which Englishmen have planted and Frenchmen have adopted in Canada, and which even in the tropics seem to withstand the enervating influence of climate.

If Imperial Federation of Britain and her colonies is to be effected, sentiment even more than self-interest must be the federating force. Sentiment will help to solve many a difficulty, and primarily that question as to the personality and function of the head of the Federation. Although no member of the Federation would create a king to preside over her local government, a constitutional monarch might appropriately be the head of the Federation. He would represent in his person the traditions of the past, and embody the historical continuity of the race. Powerless to interfere arbitrarily, but not, therefore, bereft of influence, the creature of his subjects, though nominally the controller of their fate, his right to avert injustice and enforce fair play, even if never exercised, would exert a restraining power. Such a nominal head, called by whatever name the Republican principles of the Federation would allow to be applied, would be a less dangerous and more picturesque chief than an elected president.

A far more difficult problem would be to balance the power of the executive, legislative, and judicial branches; to define the functions of the elective representatives of the Federal Council; to fairly apportion representation to it; to decide whether it should be a mere board of arbitration for the settlement of inter-state disputes and questions affecting trade and commerce, or whether it should be endowed with the higher functions of Parliament, and empowered to commit the Federation to defensive and offensive war. All these and a hundred other decisions could only be made by states of complete independent integrity, free from the dictation or the overt influence of a paramount power.

In any case, the more restricted the sphere

of Federal interference, and consequently the more complete the right of independent action by each state within its own domain, the less jealousy and friction there would be. An experiment (for experiment it necessarily will be) at Federation should aim at accomplishing as much as possible with the simplest possible machinery, leaving to the future the development of a more intricate and comprehensive system, if experience should call for it.

The most direct step ever taken towards Imperial Federation was when Lord Salisbury proposed, or rather suggested, a commercial *Zollverein* between the mother-country and her friendly children. Unfortunately the circumstance which elicited the suggestion was the adverse trade policy of England's oldest and most refractory offspring. When the North American colonies were dependencies, one of their grievances was the selfish trade and commercial policy of the mother-country. Since then the mother-country has adopted the freest trade policy ever pursued by a great nation, but her old dependencies have not unlearned some of the lessons she so emphatically impressed upon them. It is not from overt hostility but from self-interest that not only the great Republic, but most of the British colonies, refuse to follow her example. In the case of the United States, her fiscal system dictates that policy, but it has created a trade rivalry which must necessarily become more and more acute, though it need not degenerate into unfriendliness.

Half a century ago, when England saw fit to adopt the principles of free-trade, there seemed to be a leaning in the same direction on the part of the United States. Its government was then controlled by the South. The South produced cotton, of which England was by far the largest purchaser. In return for cotton, England offered the South every class of manufactures at a less cost than they could be bought at home. But the War of Secession banished all thought of any nearer approach to a common trade policy. A high tariff was imperatively forced on the country. It was imposed for purposes of revenue, but it fostered manufactures and made many rich. When the amount yielded by customs grew to be in excess of the requirements of government, the Democratic party urged reform of the tariff, and curtailment of duties. The Mills Bill, framed with this object, was defeated. The following Congress was Republican, and passed the McKinley Tariff Bill, avowedly as a measure of protection, nominally in the interest of the working masses, really in the interest of the accumulating classes.

The New York *Tribune*, during the national campaign which followed the passage of the bill, covered the first page of several issues of its weekly edition with a list of the wealthy men of the country, designating by an asterisk those who had been enriched by tariff legislation. The list was long, but it was very short compared with that of the millions who have contributed, in higher cost of living, to the wealth which has made a plutocracy of the few. It might be supposed, more appropriately, to be a campaign document of the anti-tariff party. On the contrary, it was a shrewd move to win votes, not from the workingmen, but from the average trader and small manufacturer, who, excited by the wealth which had accrued to so many, were tempted to support a system which in a few years might elevate them to the same glorious height, and cause their names to be enrolled in the McKinley peerage of money.

But while parties have been using the tariff as a party issue, the cost of government has been increasing so rapidly that the whole proceeds of even the tariff for protection are being absorbed. The pension list, let who will be responsible for its length, must be paid. A navy must be built. The appropriation for harbor and river improvements must grow greater and greater. The cost of government, already in excess of that of Great Britain, goes rolling on, and renders it practically impossible to reduce the tariff, unless resort be had to direct taxation or higher internal revenue.

But if a high tariff is to be maintained, foreign trade will be shut out, and consequently commercial intercourse will dwindle from sheer lack of exchange. To avoid this inevitable consequence, which all but the extremest protectionists recognize and admit would be a misfortune, Mr. Blaine devised a scheme of reciprocity by which other high-tariff countries should admit certain American products and manufactured articles in return for free admission into the United States of certain of their commodities, principally raw materials. When the admission of the foreign commodity injures a home industry of considerable industrial or political importance, the home interest is recompensed by a bounty. Thus Cuban and other sugars enter duty free, and the cost of sugar to the American consumer seems to have correspondingly declined. But what the sugar consumer thinks he saves, because he pays his grocer less, he pays into the Treasury as increased taxation, to reimburse the Louisiana sugar-planter for the protection of which he has been deprived!

The system has not been on trial long enough to be an assured success or an assured failure, but one thing it has done:

while it has led to reciprocity treaties between the United States and some high-tariff countries, whose exports are of raw material, it has induced other high-tariff countries, whose exports are only manufactured goods, and whose trade with the United States was certainly hampered by the McKinley Bill, to combine among themselves for mutual protection and effective recrimination. But England, consistent in her free-trade policy, stands alone and powerless. She even allows her sugar dependencies in the West Indies to enter the United States protective league. Canada has treated with her neighbor with the same object in view, but the United States must decline to admit Canadian raw material free, unless Canada will, in her tariff on manufactured articles, discriminate in her favor, which is the gist of a reciprocity treaty, and therefore against Great Britain.

If, after a fair trial, the United States finds or thinks it to be to her advantage to persist in this dual policy of high protection at home and preferential discrimination in favor of reciprocating communities abroad, and other countries follow her example, it is difficult to see how Great Britain is to defend herself, except by adopting similar tactics.

Though the drift of political opinion in the United States has veered towards a free international trade policy, the reverse has been the case in Europe, as evinced by the new German-Russian treaty and the French duty on wheat. There, however, economical conditions are complicated by, if not subordinate to, political motives, which happily do not influence us on this continent.

It is inevitable that, be their fiscal policies what they may, England and the United States are certain to be competitors in the world's markets for the sale of the great staples of the manufacturers' skill; for, despite the great growth of population in the United States, the growth of her iron and steel and of her textile-fabric industries is gradually outstripping the demands of her home market.

To divert the inevitable decline in prices

which results from overstocking the home market, every trade has organized under one form or another a trust or combination, whose efforts are directed to checking unbridled competition, and keeping within the limits of consumption the production of protected articles. Of the trusts, those are most easily managed and most successful which manipulate the movement of commodities which are the product of a limited region, such as petroleum and anthracite coal, or highly protected articles like iron and steel.

But the day inevitably comes when the laws of trade, or the cupidity of the more favored mines or mills, or the necessities of the financially embarrassed, induce some works of large capacity to overstep the artificial barrier, to produce in excess of its allowance, and thus to break faith with its partners, but not to break the law. Then commences a competitive stampede, in which each large corporation uses its plant and resources to the utmost limit of its capacity and of its credit. This they do, either impelled by ambition to stand at the head of the list, as the biggest producer, though every inch of increase means an ell less of profit, or from valid economical motives, in the endeavor to reduce the percentage of administration expenses by distributing them over a larger output.

Thus, once the control of the management of a combination is weakened, competition again comes into play, and individual folly, selfishness, or necessity brings about excessive production. That excessive product must be sold at any price, and must therefore of necessity seek a foreign market. The price of the foreign market soon comes to fix the price at home, and then protection ceases to protect. This sequence of events has already followed in the history of some protected industries in the United States, and if laws against trusts can be enforced it will be the fate of others, unless admission for protected articles be secured to other protected markets, which is the aim of the reciprocity politicians and economists. The natural resources of the Union are so vast, and the energy and ingenuity of its people so uncontrollable and keen, that production will in any case sooner or later refuse to be restricted to home consumption.

Whether, therefore, by shutting out England's manufactures from her own market by a protective tariff, or from other markets by reciprocity temptations, or whether by cheapening the cost of her own goods through a free-trade policy, and entering as a competitor on equal terms the markets of the world, the United States is sure to be England's antagonist, not, at any rate for a long time to come, her commercial ally.

Looking at the natural resources, still undeveloped and not half discovered, and the growing population of the Republic, occupying half a new continent, and looking at the little Island digging deep for its mineral wealth, and teeming with people who jostle one another for mere existence, one can hardly doubt what the issue will be, unless the little Island can gather into a commercial league, offensive and defensive, the scattered members of her family from north and south, and east and west, who still bear to her filial affection. Whether even that will avail, must depend upon the course of trade relations the world over. Yet, if the nations of the earth are to be marshalled into hostile commercial camps—as is the indication at present—legislating in their own favors as against all others, it would seem as if England and her colonies could, advantageously to its members, compose a powerful *Zollverein*, strong enough to be self-supporting, and to enforce respectful recognition of its rights by others. And should in time the policy of isolation be abandoned by the nations in favor of more cosmopolitan commercial intercourse, out of these close trade relations, which we will suppose have been harmoniously maintained by the British Federation, might grow a political partnership of still wider range, which would realize the highest aspirations of the Federalists.

But neither a commercial union of Britain and her colonies alone, nor a political federation of the whole Anglo-Saxon race, would be durable, if effected at the dictation of one or more supreme powers, or if the suspicion even existed that either was formed to subserve special local interests. Take, for instance, Canadian trade relations to the United States to-day. Reasonable as it is that Canada should not make a reciprocity treaty with the States which would discriminate against British manufacturers, it is unfortunate that her relations to the mother-country are such that she could not if she would, without the act being passed upon and possibly vetoed by the supreme power. The moral effect of Canada's refusing to do so, if perfectly free and untrammelled, would be felt appreciably on both sides of the Atlantic—as keenly in the United States as in England; whereas a vague sense of degradation of necessity accompanies the refusal in the mind of every Canadian when he feels that he is virtually obliged to consent to a course which fairness and patriotism would impel him to adopt, were he politically independent.

It is impossible to weigh the material

advantages which might accrue to Canada from commercial intercourse with the United States, as against those which might result from membership in a great confederation of other Anglo-Saxon communities capable of raising all the raw materials and manufactures that are natural to the tropics, the temperate, and the arctic zones; possessing territory teeming with an abundance of mineral wealth, and skill to turn it to account; and above all, imbued and impelled by the same love of liberty and the same faculty of adapting themselves and their principles to the most diverse conditions of existence. At the same time, this marshalling of industrial communities into hostile armies bears the semblance of a retrograde movement, seeing that for nineteen centuries the gospel of Christian communism has been in men's hands, if not in their hearts. Its fundamental principle, that "God hath made of one blood all nations of men for to dwell on all the face of the earth" (Acts xvii, 26), is as antagonistic to dynastic and national as to selfish trade aggrandizement.

CHAPTER III.

ANNEXATION AN ALTERNATIVE TO INDEPENDENCE.

WE return, therefore, to the proposition with which we set out, that independence or annexation is the alternative offered to the Canadian people, inasmuch as Imperial Federation involves Independence, and is only possible as its consequence; whereas, Annexation is a very possible sequence to Canada's present dependent position. In coming to a decision, supposing the decision to be reached by mere process of reasoning and feeling, without any outward controlling pressure, the Canadian people may be expected to be influenced by the same motives as would move an individual Canadian to accept or refuse American citizenship.

There are many Canadians and Englishmen in the United States, engaged in business and owning property, who have not taken out their naturalization papers, and therefore remain aliens in a friendly land. Why do they impose political ostracism on themselves, when, in most cases, they are in hearty sympathy with the republican institutions under which they thrive? Simply because, unable to throw off their strong attachment to their native land, they will not apply for citizenship.

Englishmen feel also that, so long as those sympathies are strong, they would be unable to act as loyal citizens of the United States in case of any quarrel between their adopted country and that of their birth; for no elderly person can so divest himself of his prejudices (if they be so) and of his affection for, or antipathy towards, the home of his forefathers, as to be a perfectly impartial citizen of another country. Many Englishmen, therefore, think they are truer to the land which has treated them generously, and that they relieve themselves from many a perplexing case of conscience, by retaining their allegiance to Great Britain and depriving themselves of certain advantages which the land of their adoption liberally offers. At the same time, living under American institutions, an Englishman enjoys the common privileges of the Anglo-Saxon race, and he feels that there is no such incongruity in making the United States his home, and seeing his children settle there and grow up into Americans, as there would be in deciding to end his days and contemplate the education and domestication and naturalization of his family in any European state.

Another reason which repels Englishmen from seeking naturalization is the bitterness expressed against England by a section of the American people, and the unfair criticisms levelled against her, and the unjust insinuations, and the imputations of unwarrantable motives with which English affairs and the relations of England to America are discussed in the American press. We know that much of this rhodomontade is but a dishonest bid for votes, and a contemptible method of increasing the sale of newspapers; but, nevertheless, the votes must be many which respectable politicians will descend to secure by such methods ; and abuse of Great Britain must be grateful to a large number of readers to induce influential journals to print the ridiculous statements and criticisms which irritate not only Englishmen but intelligent and candid Americans.

The Roman Catholic Irish population of the United States is, to a man, violently anti-British, and it is *per capita* politically the most active, and, therefore, influential, section of the people. The Germans and Scandinavians have no acute antipathy to Great Britain, but they have no sympathy with her, and were an anti-English cry raised, would readily join in it. The prevalence of this antipathy jars on the feelings of an Englishman resident in the United States, and deters him from accepting the privileges which citizenship confers.

The same feelings, excited by the same causes, undoubtedly animate a large section of the Canadian people against annexation. It may be very foolish on the part of an Englishman to deny himself the advantages and the security of property which citizenship confers, and on the part of Canada to allow sentiment to interfere with prosperity (supposing that it does), but the United States would not be the United States were it not that it owes its institutions and racial strength to that very England, whose sons to-day, while admiring it and living under its flag, and working hard to advance its prosperity, yet cling too tenaciously to the traditions of the old stock to readily disown allegiance to the mother-country; and Canada would not be Canada were it not for a large infusion of the United Empire Loyalists into the population of Ontario and the Maritime Provinces. The spirit which impelled those fugitives to forsake home and to abandon their property for an idea, and that idea patriotic affection to England, is not dead yet.

It is undeniable that in Canada itself there are groups of the population indifferent, if not hostile, to Great Britain. The Celt of Canada is a Celt still, with all his Saxon antipathies, and the French-Canadian is a Frenchman still, with religious principles, racial instincts, traditions, and memories, which tend to keep him from amalgamating into one people with the English elements of the body politic.

But these are only sections of a people which, as a whole, is loyal to England. The attitude of professional politicians towards the Anglophobists on the opposite sides of the line is suggestive. In the United States the anti-English sentiment is expressed or encouraged by party leaders and by newspapers, in order to weld into more manageable shape, for political purposes, certain classes of voters. Some Canadian politicians have tried cautiously, but found it dangerous, to use the same tactics; for while the bulk of the population on the one side of the line is loyal to England, the bulk of the population on the other is simply indifferent.

But this hostility or indifference pervades the people of the United States less widely than might be expected, and the feeling of attachment to England is extraordinarily strong, considering how dilute and remote the kinship is becoming.

The colonists who revolted numbered less than three millions,[1] and of these the Dutch of New York and the Swedes, Dutch, and Germans of Pennsylvania formed a large contingent. The white population had not increased to much above 5,000,000 when the War of 1812 embroiled the kindred peoples in hostility. Since then there have been incorporated by direct immigration three and one half millions of Irish, all cherishing grievances against the land of their expatriation; six millions of Germans, Scandinavians, and Slavs, who, if they do not harbor dislike, have brought with them from their homes a vague jealousy of Great Britain; and one and one half millions of French and French-Canadians, with whom aversion to, amounting in some to hatred of, "perfidious Albion" is an article of faith. And yet this mixed population has assimilated English ideas, has adopted the English language, and is applying in practice the essential doctrines of English political liberty and jurisprudence.

[1] The census for 1790 gives the white population at 3,172,006 and the black at 757,208.

Annexation. 41

The universal use of the English language is a most noteworthy instance of the unifying process now going on in the United States. Wherever English is spoken, it is intelligible English. In England there are dialects so different from literary English and so obscure that a cultivated native cannot understand them. But the English of America is a language which every English-thinking and -speaking person can comprehend and converse in. There are peculiarities of intonation and accentuation in the American speech; and the use of certain peculiar words and phrases distinguishes different sections, but Americans of the East understand those of the West, and those of the North understand those of the South, while a Dorsetshire peasant cannot converse with a Yorkshire man.

The universal use of the English language and consequent familiarity with English literature, coupled with closer and closer commercial and social intercourse between Old England and New England, in her expansion over the whole continent, is creating an English sentiment, and is obliterating the positively hostile feeling which was acute in 1812; which was dying out prior to the War of Secession, but which was then revived by England's staunch neutrality and the undisguised sympathy with the Southern cause of many Canadians.

In April last, when the marines and seamen of the nine fleets which anchored in New York harbor to celebrate the Columbian quadro-centennial passed through the streets of New York, a heartier and warmer welcome was shouted to the English contingent than even to the French and Russian. The seamen of the American and English fleets marched with so distinct a swing and exhibited so expressively the same air of good humor that it was impossible not to recognize a brotherhood of race, and inherited sea instincts. This co-fraternity appealed so irresistibly to the crowds of Americans of diverse origin (not half of them of American parentage) which lined the streets, that it elicited for the British tars almost as hearty cheers as those which greeted the men of the White Squadron. The parade occurred at the very time a court of arbitration was sitting in Paris to settle a dispute which, in any other age than this, or if existing between any other nations, would have been settled by force of arms.

Were Canadians to become citizens of the United States by their own will and option, there would be little seen and heard, unless they sought offence where none was meant, which would wound their love for their old home; the influence of their votes on the other hand, and still more of their moral and sentimental influence in favor of England, would add weight and impetus to the existing forces which bind in ever closer and friendlier relations the great Republic to the country which is the mother-land of us all.

Although, therefore, patriotic feeling influences, and should influence, Canadians, individually and collectively, it should not be allowed to unduly bias the decision on the question of Annexation. This should be reached dispassionately by considerations of the common good, not only financial, but political and social.

Were England in a life-and-death struggle, and did her children desert her from sordid motives, the ignominy of the act would stamp it with the opprobrium which attached to the betrayal of the Master by his perfidious disciple. But there would be nothing base or sordid in a political alliance of one branch of the Anglo-Saxon family with another, whose political institutions, if not identical, are harmonious, even though the prominent impelling motive be financial betterment; provided the rupture of the old tie be made with the full consent of the old partners.

The question therefore arises: assuming that England would consent to annexation, would Canada annexed be more prosperous, not than Canada as she now is, but than she might be if by gentle inducement, or by violent shock, she could be galvanized into greater activity than she displays to-day?

That Canada as a whole does not progress as rapidly as her neighbor, is a statistical fact, and one of such serious importance that it claims anxious investigation. Every Canadian census, till the last, has shown a healthy active growth. Now that Canada undoubtedly occupies a more important position among the communities of the world, politically, industrially, and geographically, than ever before, population ceases to flow in, or, if it flows in, it flows out again in so steady a stream that she barely maintains the normal increase that is natural to a young people with abundance of land unoccupied, and of resources undeveloped.

She exhibited between 1880 and 1890 a power of attracting and absorbing population equal to only half of that of her neighbor. In this comparison lies the most perplexing and disquieting feature of the question: for if the United States continues growing into a giant, while Canada shrinks into a dwarf, with the distorted and unhealthy impulses which affect people, as well as individuals, of impaired development, the result can be easily forecast.

CHAPTER IV.

CANADA'S SLOW PROGRESS (COMPARED WITH THAT OF AUSTRALIA AND THE UNITED STATES) DUE TO PHYSICAL CONDITIONS.

THE growth of population in Canada has not even reached a high standard of natural increase, and therefore the 800,000 who have entered as immigrants, during the last decennial period, have about compensated for an equal number of immigrants, composed in part of those same immigrants, who merely passed through Canada, but principally of Canadians, who left to seek their fortunes elsewhere, most, but not all, in the United States.

The decennial increase of the following European nations between 1860 and 1870 was calculated by a Commission of French savants, into whose table I insert the percentage growth of the United States and

Canada between 1880 and 1890. These figures are in most cases higher than those arrived at by Bodio.

			Per cent.	Per cent. per annum.	Bodio.
United States,	between	1880 and 1890..	24.8 or	2.48	
Russia	do	1860 and 1870..	13.9	1.39	1.11
Sweden	do	do ..	13.3	1.33	1.15
England & Wales	do	do ..	12.6	1.26	1.24
Prussia	do	do ..	12.6	1.26	.98
Canada	do	1880 and 1890..	11.6	1.16	
Italy	do	1860 and 1870..	8.3	.83	.71
Spain	do	do ..	6.7	.67	.35
France	do	do ..	3.8	.38	.35

None of these countries, except the United States and Canada, was notably affected by immigration, though some lost heavily by emigration. Canada thus stands at the foot of the class of nations of healthy growth. Considering the prolific habits of the French Canadian peasantry, she should stand higher from natural increase alone.

She should be the compeer of Australia and the United States, for they and Canada for several decades have been the magnetic centres to which the world's surplus population has been attracted. Of the three, Australia has grown the most rapidly.

Comparing the population of her constituent colonies and of New Zealand and Tasmania in 1871, 1881, and 1891, we find the decennial gain in population to have been as follows:

	1871.	1881.	Per cent. gain.	1891.	Per cent. gain.
New Zealand	256,393	489,933	90.9	626,658	20.8
Victoria	731,528	862,346	17.8	1,140,405	32.2
South Australia	185,626	279,865	50.8	320,430	18.0
New South Wales	503,981	751,468	49.1	1,132,230	52.0
Queensland	120,104	213,525	77.7	393,718	84.3
Western Australia	25,353	29,708	17.1	49,782	67.5
Tasmania	101,785	115,705	13.4	146,667	26.7

The total population of the above colonies was in 1871, 1,924,770, and in 1891, 3,809,890. Their growth in 20 years was 97.9 per cent. or 4.8 per cent. per annum. The colony of Victoria had, in 1891, 12.9 inhabitants per square mile to 20.6 in the United States, and 1.42 in Canada.

There is no doubt of the inaccuracy of the results of the United States census for several decades past. Apart from the errors in local enumeration, the Census Bureau itself discredits the reliability of the census of 1870, and wishes to revise the

Canada's Slow Progress.

totals. Taking the figures as they stand, the population of the United States was in—

		Decennial. Per cent. gain.
1860	31,443,321	....
1870	38,558,371	22.6
1880	50,155,783	30.0
1890	62,622,250	24.8

As revised for 1870, the totals would stand :

		Decennial. Per cent. gain.
1860	31,443,321	...
1870	39,818,449	26.6
1880	50,155,783	25.9
1890	62,622,250	24.8

The population of Canada during the same period shows the following fluctuations :

		Decennial. Per cent. gain.
1861	3,171,418	....
1871	3,686,596	16.2
1881	4,324,810	17.3
1891	4,829,411	11.6

Australia has, therefore, grown more rapidly than any of the other offshoots of the Anglo-Saxon stock. Though her total population is comparatively small, and the actual increment has been only about 8 per cent. of that of the United States, nevertheless her marvellous vitality would seem conclusively to contradict the assumption that her colonial form of government has had a repellent influence on immigration. While the socialistic tendency of Australian legislation may have had an attraction for such intelligent immigrants as have been able to meet the cost of a voyage to the antipodes, the inference nevertheless is that emigrants in general are not prejudiced in favor of one form of representative government over another, provided there be full liberty of self-government. If this be so, Canada is not deserted because she is a colony, but for other reasons.

There are points of resemblance between Australia and the United States, and points of difference between Canada and Australia, which may help to explain the stagnation of immigration into Canada.

Climate is a potent factor in determining immigration. Between Southern New Zealand and Northern Queensland, there is a wider range of temperature than between Texas and Maine. Though New Zealand has the mean temperature of Eastern New York, the northern half of Australia is in the tropics. In spite of the aridity of Australia, the freedom from extreme cold has undoubtedly its effect on the fancy of the immigrant. And no wonder ! for half the energies of the population of Quebec and Manitoba, and no small share of its wealth, are expended in keeping itself warm and battling with snow and ice.

Of the direct effect of climate, the United States census gives many an example. For instance its rigorous climate is doubtless the reason why Maine,—

	Per cent.
between 1860 and 1870, declined	0.22
between 1870 and 1880, increased only	3.51
between 1880 and 1890, increased only	1.87

while North Carolina, with as poor a soil, and but few manufactures, even during the war period,—

	Per cent.
from 1860 to 1870, gained	1.9
from 1870 to 1880, gained	30.6
from 1880 to 1890, gained	15.5

Mineral wealth is as potent a factor as climate in determining the current of immigration.

The tremendous waves of population which flow into a district under the influence of speculative mining nearly doubled the population of Colorado between 1870 and 1880, and more than doubled the population of Montana between 1880 and 1890. Both these States, like California, had other resources than mines, which resources those who failed in mining turned their hands to developing, and have thus created communities with permanent and stable industries.

Australia, under like physical conditions, has experienced similar accessions to its population. Though the absence of such vast tracts of fertile land as have drawn so much of the surplus population of the world to the prairies of the West, will of necessity limit the number which Australia can ultimately accommodate, her very aridity has facilitated the discovery of minerals, and been the prime mover thither of population. In a barren, treeless region, where the rocks are exposed, minerals, if they exist, are easily and rapidly discovered.

The surprising speed with which the mining of precious metals drew the hardiest and most enterprising of the reckless spirits of the world to California, after 1848, was almost exceeded during the next decade in the experience of Australia. Of the multitudes who then and have since flocked to both scenes of mining excitement, the major part, disappointed in their search for fortune beneath the soil, have, in despair, turned their energies to cattle ranching or agriculture, and created large communities of people, far above the average in intelligence and enterprise.

Canada has undoubtedly mineral wealth, but nature has very carefully hidden it, as if to save it for future generations and prevent its reckless exhaustion. The Canadian Rocky Mountains are probably as richly impregnated with gold and silver as the same ranges south of the line, but they are heavily clad with soil and forest. Exploration is therefore difficult, discovery is slow, and the enthusiasm of the prospector seldom reaches that white heat which precedes and creates a " rush."

These reasons may explain why the Eastern Provinces of Canada make no better progress than Maine, and why British Columbia does not keep pace with Montana. The United States has heretofore won most of her immigrants by offering them high wages in her mines and manufactories, or by presenting them with cheap, rich lands in a temperate zone. Canada has not, and cannot, hold out similar or equal inducements, and therefore till wages fall in the United States, and the more desirable lands are absorbed, it is unlikely that Canada will keep pace with her neighbor.

CHAPTER V.

IF THE "NATIONAL" OR PROTECTION POLICY HAS FAILED TO ATTRACT POPULATION TO CANADA, WILL ANNEXATION DO SO?

CANADA cannot attract a large manufacturing population, because she cannot give it work. The reason why she cannot, is not far to seek. The most palpable cause for the languishing state of certain manufactures in Canada is the want of a large home market. Applying high duties keeps out foreign goods, and secures the home market to the home manufactures. If the home market be big enough, the policy works admirably for the manufacturer and the operative. Dear goods can afford to pay costly labor, and all are happy but the consumer, who has to buy the dear goods. If the consumers are numerous enough to support extensive industries, and the industries by means of trusts and combinations restrict their production to the home demand, the manufacturer heaps up wealth, certain groups of the laboring classes are well paid, and people in certain sections are prosperous. The whole train of consequences follows the protective policy of the United States, because the home market is so large, and is ever growing.

It did not follow the protective National Policy in Canada, because the market was too restricted to allow of manufacturing on a scale which would employ enough of her native population to raise wages to anything like the standard in the Eastern and Western States. No immigrant was tempted to enter Canada from abroad by the offer of high wages, and no Canadian was restrained from migrating by the offer of even equal wages at home to those that tempted him in the Eastern and Western States.

If, therefore, the National Policy has failed to produce all the results which were anticipated from it, will absolute reciprocity confer the coveted benefit? If mills have not been built, and population has not flowed in to work them, because Canada has only 5,000,000 of people to clothe and house, would her lot be better were she coupled up with her 63,000,000 of neighbors? We doubt it.

Maine is within the charmed circle. It has lumber in abundance, and water power runs to waste in a hundred rivers, but the population of Maine by the last census shows an increase of only 1.8 per cent. in 10 years. But Maine is as cold as Quebec, her soil is poor, and the labor of reclaiming it oppressive.

At the same time that the higher wages which have prevailed through active manufacturing in some sections of the United States have attracted immigrants, the abundance and cheapness of land in a temperate climate has been another temptation. Canada also possesses boundless land which is open to occupation, under the Homestead Act, as freely as that in the United States; but the unoccupied lands of Quebec and Ontario are uninviting, and the prairie lands of the Northwest are repellently cold. The movement of population in North Dakota exemplifies the aversion of the immigrant to cold, and the risk which it entails. Dakota is Manitoba's neighbor to the south, and the statistical returns from that State are particularly instructive :

Between 1880 and 1890 North Dakota grew from 36,909 to 182,719 or 393.05 per cent.; South Dakota from 98,268 to 328,-808 or 234.60 per cent. ; considered as one, from 135,177 to 511,527 or 278.46 per cent.

But in 1885 a territorial census was made. It showed that the Dakotas then contained 415,610 inhabitants, and therefore exhibited growth between 1880 and 1885 of 207.4 per cent., and between 1885 and 1890 of only 26.7 per cent. Evidently, therefore, climatic conditions have disappointed the Dakotan farmer as well as the Manitoban.

In the old prairie States where land is no longer obtainable for the mere asking, rapid growth has of necessity ceased. The following paragraph from the compendium of the *Eleventh United States Census*, p. xli, is worthy of study:

"In Ohio, Indiana, Iowa, and Missouri, and in Illinois, if the city of Chicago be dropped out of consideration, the rate of increase has declined very decidedly. In Ohio it has fallen from 19.99 to 14.83 per cent. In Indiana from 17.71 to 10.82 per cent. In Iowa from 36.06 to 17.68 per cent. In Missouri from 25.97 to 23.56 per cent., in spite of the rapid growth of St. Louis and Kansas City; and in Illinois, dropping Chicago from consideration, from 14.89 to 5.9 per cent. In these States the agricultural industry, which is still the prominent one, has begun to decline owing to the sharp competition of western farms."

But, despite this sharp competition, we have seen that Dakota, the newest and most vigorous of these western rivals, has ceased growing with phenomenal rapidity, and Kansas, the most powerful, according to the State census, accumulated two thirds of her decennial gain during the first half of the decade, and during the last year of the decade actually lost 37,818 of her inhabitants. The same is true, though to a less startling extent, of Minnesota. That rich prairie State, which has not yet begun to feel the impoverishment of its fertile lands, " increased 77.57 per cent. between 1870 and 1880 and 66.74 per cent. between 1880 and 1890, the numerical increase being over half a million in the past decade. The State census taken in 1885 showed that the bulk of this increase occurred between 1880 and 1885. The numerical increase during the first five years was 337,025 and the rate of increase 43.17 per cent., while during the last half of the decade the numerical increase was 184,028, and the rate of increase 16.46 per cent." (compendium of the *Eleventh United States Census*, p. xli). The climate of the Canadian Northwest under the shelter of the Rocky Mountains being milder than the United States Territories immediately south of the line, and good arable land in abundance being still open to homesteaders there is a small but steady stream of immigrants across the border northward.

Returning to the statistical summary given above, the manipulated figures show a percentage decline in the growth of the United States between 1880 and 1890 of 1.1 per cent., but following the actual returns, the decline was 5.22 per cent. Compared with the previous decennial period, the decline for the corresponding period in Canada was 5.65 per cent. Of course we do not pretend that a percentage decline of equal amount from such different aggregates as the population of Canada and the United States is equally portentous to both, but a decline in both cases may mark the turning-point in the movement of population to this continent. Naturally the decline will be more marked in the less favored region, and taken as a whole and all in all, Canada is less favored than the United States. In point of fact the actual volume of immigration to the United States is not rapidly declining. The percentage volume is, however, shrinking, and the quality and destination of the immigrants are changing most notably. From the report on immigration published by the Treasury Department of the United States in 1891 we extract the following figures which show conclusively the source whence future immigration will be chiefly drawn.

	Arrivals in the U. S. in 1869.	Arrivals in the U. S. in 1890.
Austria-Hungary	1,495	29,632
Germany	131,042	92,427
Great Britain	43,434	69,790
Ireland	40,786	53,024
Italy	1,489	52,003
Norway	16,068	11,370
Poland	184	11,073
Russia	343	33,147
Finland	0	2,451
Sweden	24,224	29,632
Switzerland	3,650	6,993
Total Europe	315,543	443,225
British America	21,117 and in 1885	35,291

The report gives the number of immigrants from British America between 1873 and 1885 at 688,813. Since 1885 the law has made no provisions for taking count of immigrants entering the United States by land.

This large influx of Poles, Slavs and Italians settles in the seaboard cities, and in the iron, coal, and coke regions. Italians have largely replaced the Irish as streetsweepers and railroad navvies, and Poles furnish the hands with which the iron and coal magnates have opposed the demands of the native laborers. There has been a decrease in the introduction of skilled labor and good farmers, and an increase in the number of unskilled immigrants, who cannot and do not combine to maintain a standard of wages. The result, if this state of things continues, will be, not only that the intellectual status of the electorate will be lowered, but the standard of wages paid for unskilled labor will sink and the temptation to indiscriminate immigration will be lessened.

To sum up, Canada can offer no inducement to foreigners to operate her manufactories, which were and will be few till her population is large enough to absorb the product of many, or till she seeks a foreign market, for she has a surplus of cheap labor at home. Her wild forest lands are too difficult to reclaim, and too slow in supporting the farmer, to be occupied while there is any prairie land unappropriated.

Her prairie lands lie north of the favored zone, and, as in the case of her neighbor Dakota, are less eagerly coveted, when their climate has been experienced, than lands to the south. British Columbia, unfortunately, comprises within her bounds so little agricultural land, that were every acre of it occupied, the growth of population could not be a tithe of that of the State of Washington; and British Columbia's mineral wealth is so hidden by forest and soil, that though a large contingent of American prospectors are searching for it, discovery is of necessity far slower than in the contiguous States of Montana and Idaho. These natural disadvantages attach to her, as they do to Maine and North Dakota. Her political condition or affiliations do not affect them.

Canada must, therefore, face the fact that she has serious physical and geographical obstacles to contend against, and be content to make haste slowly. This, after all, is a lesser evil than being overrun by a large horde of ignorant alien immigrants.

CHAPTER VI.

PROBABLE EFFECT OF ANNEXATION ON CANADIAN INDUSTRIES AND WAGES.

There are good and substantial reasons why Canada's progress in population should be less than that of her neighbor, but there is no good reason why it should be so slow as it is. There is in Canada a latent suspicion that something is wrong, but instead of seeking for the source of her shortcomings at home, in her own habits and business methods, she is prone to charge them wholly to external causes, and to look for a remedy in political changes. To some minds, and at one time or another to some leaders of almost all the political groups, annexation has been the panacea.

Assuming that annexation were effected, whence would result the magical improvement in Canada's financial position which some anticipate from it? Canada's public debt was in 1890 much larger (per capita) than that of the United States, being $67.81 per head as against $14.24. The difference in the event of annexation would have to be distributed among and borne by the annexed States and added to the expenses of State government, which would not be less than those of supporting the Provincial governments now are. The system of State taxation would, moreover, have to be revised, as there would be no contribution by the Federal government for the maintenance of the States. The more impecunious States would then whine in vain for better terms when in financial straits.

It is questionable whether manufacturing in general would be stimulated by annexation. There is a tendency towards segregation in manufacturing industries directed by influences which it is not always easy to detect. The cotton mills of the United States were first attracted to certain localities in New England by water power, and though they have grown beyond the capacity of the water power, they still remain, because capital has been invested, and skilled labor has congregated there, though the material is brought to the mills from the other end of the Union. So, likewise, nearly all of the copper of the United States is converted into manufactured articles in the Naugatuck Valley, though Connecticut itself produces no copper, and reships a large proportion of the manufactured goods back over the roads by which the raw material reached her. Woollen manufacturing is largely localized near Philadelphia, though Pennsylvania raises comparatively little wool. If manufacturers went to the cheap labor centres, all the cotton mills would be removed to the South, where the raw material is raised, and where labor is cheaper by far than it is in Canada. But though a cotton mill, in rivalry with the North, is springing up here and there throughout the Southern States, the cotton manufacturing trade remains immovable where it has long been located, and where economically it ought not to be, far from raw material, from cheap labor, and from fuel.

What likelihood is there, therefore, that mills would be built in Canada to employ the hands who now flock to New England? This labor would continue to go from the State of Quebec, instead of from the Province of Quebec, to the States of Maine, Connecticut, Rhode Island, or Massachusetts. The mills would remain where the mills are now, and labor would go to the mills, not the mills to the labor.

There are special branches of manufacture which at first sight it would seem should be carried on in Canada. She possesses far vaster resources in lumber than the United States. They are now being used as rapidly, perhaps more so than is prudent; but the lumber leaves Canada in an unmanufactured shape. A minimum of labor and skill has therefore been expended on it. When it reaches its destination across the line, it is converted into special forms for special uses. Prosperous towns have grown up on the southern shores of the great lakes, whose main industry is turning Michigan and Canadian lumber into furniture and architectural decorations.

But these manufacturing centres are nearer their market than any point in Canada would be. As it is much cheaper to transport lumber in the rough than furniture, and as so little of the raw material is now wasted, it is very doubtful whether, under any circumstances, the furniture manufacturing trade could be shifted from the consumer to the forest. Canada's true policy is to turn her fine hard woods into specialized forms for other markets than the United States, and that she could do to-day as well as imported energy would do it for her after annexation.

Mining would doubtless be more active under annexation than it is at present, provided the United States protective tariff remains in force, but this is a proviso that it is dangerous to count upon. The existing duty of 75 cents per ton on coal is sufficient to exclude Nova Scotia and Cape Breton coals from the New England market, and secure the fuel supply to Pennsylvania. Were it removed, New England would take vastly more coal from the Maritime Provinces than she did before the expiration of Lord Elgin's Reciprocity Treaty, and would much more than compensate for the loss of the Ontario market, which would in case of annexation or reciprocity become the perquisite of Pennsylvania. But sooner or later the duty will be removed from all raw material, and these trade benefits will accrue to Canada without any change in her political status. American capitalists, anticipating this contingency, have already invested largely in Maritime coal.

The same is true of iron ores. Canadian iron manufacturing has not prospered. Why? Because it is said the home market was too small, the English market was too cheap, and the United States market was closed. All which is only partly true. The attempt at manufacturing iron on a large scale has been made at Londonderry and more recently at Ferrona, Nova Scotia, but though the government has offered all the assistance that it dared in the way of bounty and high tariff, Canada in 1891, made only 21,772 tons of pig-iron, though her consumption of iron and steel in all forms was estimated as equivalent to over 500,000 tons of pig. If her iron-ore resources are what they are supposed to be, why is not this 500,000 tons of pig, of wrought iron and steel, made with her own coal, out of her own ores, and by her own people? Why were $2,000,000 worth of foreign iron and steel imported? If the material for manufacturing be there, with the benefits of a protected market, all that would seem to be lacking is the capital, energy, and skill necessary to supply the market with the material. Pictou County, Nova Scotia, is the only spot on the Atlantic coast where coal, iron ore, and flux exist side by side on tide-water, but Canadian enterprise has not yet exerted itself to even determine whether the iron-ore deposits are of workable extent, despite Sir William Dawson's reiterated opinion as to their apparent value. Doubtless, were Canada annexed, American energy would soon determine the point, but is it creditable to Canadians thus to shift their responsibility, because they dread the risks, to Yankee shoulders and Yankee pockets?

The principal copper deposits in Canada are now in the hands of Americans, namely, the pyrites mines near Lennoxville, in the Province of Quebec, and the largest of the nickel-copper ore mines of Sudbury, in the Province of Ontario. The same is true of Canada's lead resources. Americans risked their money and failed on Lake Temiscamingue, and Americans have bought the immense lead deposits of Lake Kootenay in British Columbia. These will be developed regardless of reciprocity or annexation; and if the duty be removed from lead ores entering the United States, they will be introduced in the raw state into the United States as though they had been produced on American territory. Thus the profits will go to those who take the risks, not to the Canadians who clamor for annexation that they may more readily sell their birthright. If Canada were annexed, or should reciprocity be secured, mining would receive an impulse, and more Canadians would be employed on wage-work, for the foreign corporations who would reap the profits, if any accrue, which must to-day redound to Canadian enterprise, were it willing to jeopardize a little of its capital.

It must be, however, remembered that the removal of protective duties from ore and metals entering the United States, should this be one of the results of tariff reform, will reduce their price to the level which they command in the European market, and therefore to a lower price than they command to-day in the protected market of Canada. The economical questions involved in reciprocity or annexation are much more complicated and far-reaching than at first appears. Canada has refused to follow the lead of her mother-country as a Free-Trader. Should she ally herself with the United States politically, she would have only one-twelfth interest influence in determining her own future fiscal policy, and must obey the will of her dominant sister States, whether they be in the direction of Free Trade or Protection, and it probably will not be towards the latter.

Passing from mining and metallurgical to agricultural interests, it is undeniable that the nearest market to most sections of Canada is the United States, and that the prices are higher in New York than in Montreal, but the farmer does not always get his fair share of that higher price. Cereals are produced in excess of consumption by both countries. Only one of the cereals raised in Canada is largely purchased and used in the States, and that is barley. The McKinley Bill injured Canada by imposing a heavier duty on that grain. This imposition was not generally popular, and in any revision of the tariff the duty will probably be reduced.

The following figures, giving the United States and Canadian agricultural staples to Great Britain are more conclusive than a volume of arguments. The United States supplied England in 1890 with wheat of the value of $33,508,762; Canada supplied her with only $2,250,568. Clearly the United States would therefore not be a good customer for Canadian wheat. The United States sent to England in 1890 $19,385,815 worth of beef; Canada sent her only $367,770 worth. The United

States shipped $35,365,784 worth of horned cattle; Canada shipped only $204,640. Thus the New York market does not stand in need of Canadian beef, and would pay no more for it than the export value, no matter what the retail price of beef may be to the New York housekeeper.

The shipment made of bacon and hams to Great Britain in 1890 by the United States was of the value of $36,327,221; Canada supplied $3,742,258. In these three articles of largest agricultural production the United States and Canada produced largely in excess of their own consumption, and neither is, therefore, a profitable market for the products of the other. The foreign market, in which both compete, would consume neither more nor less, nor pay a higher price for the supply from the North American Continent, whether it be politically under one or two governments.

What Canada can do is well exemplified in her cheese industry. In 1890 she shipped to England $9,303,167 worth, equal to $1.92 per head of the population, whereas the United States shipped only

$10,116,313 worth, equal to only 16 cents per head of her population. One would naturally expect that the butter shipment would be in the same proportion, but Canada shipped only one fifth as much butter, namely $295,774 worth, as was shipped by the United States, whose shipments amounted to $1,566,791. Why should England import over $20,000,000 worth of butter from Denmark, and only $300,000 worth from Canada? One reason is that Canada's butter is so slovenly packed and so unreliable in quality, that it could nowhere command high prices. Throughout the West Indies, South America and South Africa, there is an almost unlimited market for butter, packed in tin cans at a fabulous price ; but it must be of the finest quality. That butter Canada should, but does not, supply.

London is as accessible a market for Canadian eggs as is New York, yet England pays France $6,000,000 annually for eggs, and her own colonies offer her only $50,000, or not 1 per cent. of what she buys from France. The wider channel is nowadays no greater an obstacle to commerce than the narrow one. What the Canadian farmers want is not a market, but energy, skill, and industry with which to compete in the world's market with their more pushing neighbors or more thrifty rivals. Annexation might result in an infusion of energy. It might lead to a transfer of the land from the lethargic to the more industrious. Probably it would leave matters precisely where they are, for New England has been abandoned by her farmer class in the mad rush for the West, and deserted homesteads by the hundred are waiting to be reoccupied, which are nearer the large city markets of the coast than any Canadian farms.

The fishermen of the Maritime Provinces would profit by reciprocity or annexation, but they do not make the best of the market within their own reach. Long after the Intercolonial railroad was opened, the Lower Canadian market was supplied with frozen fish, not by Nova Scotia over that road, but by the State of Maine over the Grand Trunk.

Annexation would probably improve the financial status of the territory represented by Canada, but it would improve the financial condition of the Canadians themselves, only if they yielded to the impulses which would reach them from across the line. These, if they did not push them *on*, would push them *out*. But is there not inherent activity enough in Canada to render such external impulses unnecessary, and cannot one section react on another as effectually as it is thought American go-aheadativeness would overcome the inertia of sluggishness which characterizes certain communities in the Dominion? Cannot the Scotch of Ontario infuse into the Scotch of Nova Scotia some of those qualities which have made Ontario the *only* prosperous and contented province in the Dominion, as wealthy and progressive as any similarly situated area in the United States?

It is doubtful, therefore, whether Canada would gain by annexation financially more than her own people can win by their own will and wits, if they exert them. The market of the world is the arena in which both communities must compete for the sale of the same articles which both now produce in excess, and of which Canada's resources are vast enough to make her prosperous, if her people only make good use of them.

In addition to a better market for the fruit of his toil, which tempts the farmer to try, as a remedy, a change of dynasty, better wages are promised the laboring man. It is natural that the wage question should influence the opinion of the bulk of the people. Were it certain that a political change, involving none of the degradation of conquest, would double a man's income, there is very little doubt how his vote would be cast on any political issue involving that consequence. The argument is freely used that annexation or intimate fiscal union with the United States will at once raise the standard of wages in Canada to that of the United States. But what is the United States standard? There is in fact none. Wages there, as elsewhere, are determined by the quantity of the supply in any given place at any given time. At present unskilled labor commands from $1.25 to $1.50 along the seaboard of the North and Middle States, but in some of the crowded manufacturing centres in Eastern Pennsylvania it can be had abundantly for $1.10. In the Southern States it is worth much less. In the more Western prairie States and in Colorado, which are accessible, and are therefore being filled to the point where labor competition is operative, wages have sunk to the level of the Eastern seaboard, while in the thinly peopled Territories and the Rocky Mountain States, $2.50 has heretofore been the current price of unskilled labor. Across the Sierra Nevada, in the more populated States of California and Oregon, unskilled labor has with difficulty commanded Eastern prices.

The cost of living influences the price of labor, chiefly because, where the cost of living is high, the poor cannot congregate and labor is consequently comparatively scarce. Moreover, when commercial depression prevails and employment is scarce, the price of labor sympathizes. For years during the depression subsequent to the panic of 1873, some of the most arduous labor in Pennsylvania was paid only 75 cents per day.

It is therefore by no means certain, for instance, that the French Canadian in the Province of Quebec would get any more after annexation than before. He is at present, to the operative of the Eastern States, what the Chinaman is to the Western laborer, the intractable, uncombinable, depressing element in the labor market of the New England States. If, after annexation, he went away from his home to the centres of industrial activity, then, as now, he would be heartily welcomed and readily employed by the manufacturer who is at issue with his old hands, and for whom he will work at wages and under conditions which others have refused, or at any rate resisted. But in his French Canadian village the wages would remain just as much below the average of that which he obtains in the factories of New England, or in the brickyards of the Hudson, as the wages in some of the more remote counties of Pennsylvania, and in the agricultural region of the South, are below those which prevail in the cities of Philadelphia and New York.

CHAPTER VII.

ANNEXATION FROM THE STANDPOINT OF COMPARATIVE POLITICS.

LOOKING at the question from a political point of view, the adoption of a new constitution presupposes a belief that the new is better than the old. Assuming that some change must be made either by choice or under force of circumstances, will Canada retain in its new constitution the main features of the British system of representative government, or that worked out by the framers of the United States constitution? If Canada is satisfied with government by a responsible Ministry and an all-powerful Lower House, she had better work out her destiny by modifying that plan of government to meet her peculiar conditions, rather than by adopting the constitution of her neighbor.

Already the Canadian constitution embodies some of the features of that of the United States. It approaches that of the United States by recognizing in the Governor-General a chief executive, whose term of office is transitory instead of being permanent. The Canadian constitution differs from that of the United States by reducing the autonomous independence of the Provinces by making them in financial matters to a certain degree dependent on the Federal Treasury, and of course in curtailing the functions of the head of the State to a nominal control, under the dictation of the chief of the party in power. That the Governor should remain a nominee of the Crown is impossible. That instead he should be a President elected for a short term will not, in view of the oft recurring disturbance of the presidential year across the line, approve itself to the Canadian people, when a new constitution is under discussion.

That whatever the term of office or manner of selection be, the head of the State should be endowed with as arbitrary power as the President, would jar on the constitutional habits of Canadians; and it would seem to them a departure from purely democratic methods, to forego the satisfaction and advantage of questioning publicly on the floor of the House, as to the management of their offices, those into whose hands they have entrusted the responsibilities of government. In England, in the United States, and in Canada, the mode of election or selection, of the members of the Upper Chamber, and the assignment of functions to its members have been the most difficult problems for solution by constitution makers.

The English House of Lords is recruited from the best men of the kingdom, and enjoys the presence of the heads of the established Church of England, who, however, under the awe of their hereditary colleagues, fail to express their opinions as freely and emphatically in the House, as in the Pulpit. But owing to its hereditary character, in these days of popular government, it never ventures to use to their full extent its delegated powers, and under no circumstances could it be duplicated or even imitated in one of England's Democratic offshoots.

The United States Senate is pointed to as the masterpiece of American constitution builders. Each State sending two Senators, irrespective of population, asserts the supremacy of the Federal principle, and the Senate, being endowed with executive functions, serves as a check on the Executive, and prevents the abuse of his wide and arbitrary power by the President. While the United States consisted of a group of well organized communities, whose legislators were composed of the best men each State could elect, the selection of Senators by such State Legislatures generally resulted in the appointment of two men as fit for the high office as could be found. But of late nearly all of the Territories have been endowed with Statehood, and thus Nevada with its 45,000 inhabitants, Idaho with 84,000, Wyoming with 60,000, send each two Senators to Washington, though they are entitled to but one Representative apiece in the Lower

House. The members of the Legislatures of the Rocky Mountain States, elected by a scanty population scattered over enormous tracts of wilderness, to whom the selection of the Senators is entrusted, do not feel sufficiently the responsibility of choosing even the best man within the range of their vision, small as that is, but are influenced by considerations not always the most patriotic and lofty. The Senators thus elected are liable to take narrow views of national politics, and to combine to force local issues on their colleagues.

It is significant that at the same time there should be dissatisfaction with both the United States Senate and the British House of Lords. Did the American people put more confidence in the legislators they send to their State and Federal legislative assemblies, a proposal to curtail the powers of the President and the Senate, and increase that of the Lower House, might be considered, as well as that of merely changing the mode of Senatorial election; but there is such a widespread and growing distrust of their popular assemblies, that all the new States in their constitutions embody as organic law what in England and her colonies is confided to the legislators.

The United States Senate was as cunningly devised a balance-wheel to the machine of state as human ingenuity ever conceived, but during the past century many changes have taken place. Federal power has grown and State influence has declined. The thirteen States, peopled by a homogeneous race of kindred habits, who had worked out in their several colonies the problems of self-government, which they were now to apply in a more complex form on a wider field, have grown into forty-four States, with many clashing interests, and peopled by a most heterogeneous population. The United States Senate, as a part of the American system, was as useful an Upper Chamber as could have been devised, but it is doubtful whether the framers of the Constitution, if doing their work afresh to-day, would distribute the Senators so unequally as to population, even in recognition of the Federal principle;

and certainly none of the Anglo-Saxon communities would follow closely the American precedent in this respect. The Canadian Senate, composed of men appointed by the Crown for life, has departed from the United States model, but it is not likely to find imitators.

In fact when we cast our glance over the many pieces of machinery devised by men, through which the essential features of the representative system are applied to the production of government, we see how faulty is the best, and what a field there is for improvement, and even invention. But improvement is most rapid when many minds are at work in solving the same problems, and therefore the more communities there are intelligently endeavoring to elaborate political systems on the general lines of self-government, through popular representation, the better.

England, despite her reputed conservatism, has been experimenting in a distinct direction, that of delegating legislative powers to even smaller sections than the States of the Union. She has seen no necessity to endow them with such autonomous rights as those claimed by the States, which rights would never have been asserted or granted had not the States possessed them before associating themselves in a federation for mutual intercourse and defence. No concrete power voluntarily submits to disintegration, and no Parliament voluntarily deprives itself of functions such as those original colonies reserved. Nevertheless, the United States, despite the rigidity of their Constitution, have amended it, and, as experience shows the necessity of further change to meet changing circumstances, will continue to amend it. In fact the Federal and State Legislatures are so many political laboratories in which are being tried many heroic political and social experiments, some of which are so dangerous that they would blow the whole fabric speedily into atoms were it not that the common sense, the high average intelligence, and the fidelity of the experimenters to the fundamental principles of representative government check revolutionary action.

In the Australasian group of the Anglo-Saxon communities the legislative experiments are being made diametrically in the direction of communism, so far with rather disastrous financial results. At the same time the ultimate result of State ownership and control of lands, mines, and railroads, as attempted by some of the Australasian colonies, on taxation and national prosperity should be watched with eager interest.

State ownership of railroads and other public works, involving an enormous and onerous public debt, was probably the most immediate cause of the recent Australian bank crisis. Its effects, however, remind us how intimate is the relation of all the great commercial communities to one another, and how sensitively all feel any reverse in prosperity which overtakes one of their number. The Australasian colonies borrowed too lavishly in England to build public works in excess of the immediate demand. A general bank failure followed, which involved a large volume of British capital. To meet urgent demands England sold American securities which had to be paid for by the United States. Their value fell and the balance of exchange was disturbed. Gold flowed across the Atlantic. This aggravated the feeling of distrust already prevailing in America, and fanned distrust into a panic. The reflection rises: " What would be the effect on the national revenue and credit of the United States if, owning all the railroads, the tremendous losses that the existing crisis has imposed on the American railroad companies and their property had fallen on the government?"

The Anglo-Saxon is steadily moving northward from the Cape of Good Hope over the whole of South Africa. Under the impetus of diamond and gold discovery, the old sleepy communities of Cape Colony and Natal are themselves waking up, and being involved with the Boer republics of the Transvaal and South Africa in a widespread confederation which must inevitably adopt a form of responsible government differing widely in its features from any yet devised. Already Englishmen are outnumbering the Dutch on Dutch territory, but find nothing uncongenial in the essential features of republican government. The Transvaal is already under a certain vague British protectorate, which seems to satisfy the national sympathies of the English colonists and miners settled there. Erelong the mineral and agricultural resources of Mashonaland and Matabeleland, stretching away to the north and northwest, will fill these wilds with Englishmen and a sprinkling of Americans. The influences of adjacent republicanism will probably shape somewhat the constitution of the new state and create a more or less distinct system of representative government. The indifference of Englishmen and even of the Imperial government to the special form of representative government under which Englishmen shall live is curiously illustrated in the recent convention between the British and Transvaal Governments for the cession of Swaziland to the Transvaal. Article V. provides: "Every white male who shall have been a *bona-fide* resident in Swaziland (even if temporarily absent from Swaziland) on the

20th of April, 1893, shall become and be entitled to all the political privileges of a full burgher of the South African Republic, as though he had been born in that Republic."

Even India, as it grows out of the state of governmental dependence under which it has heretofore necessarily existed, with its hundreds of millions of natives of diverse race, social habit, and religious belief, and its handful of alien Englishmen, leavening the vast mass with Western political and social ideas, will evolve still another and more original departure from the primitive type of British representative government.[1]

---

[1] Will not also India create a new phase of Christianity? Christianity is an Eastern religion; its writings are full of Eastern imagery, addressed to Eastern thought, and which must convey to the Eastern mind very different impressions to what they convey to the Western. Its poetry has been confused with its facts by matter-of-fact Western theologians, and both have been interpreted by the Western Church in conformity with Roman law. This interpretation, with lesser variations, has been formulated into a metaphysical conception of Christianity, which is assumed by the Western Church to be Christianity itself, and as such is presented to the Oriental. He refuses to accept it. When the writings of the New Testament, freed from Western gloss and commentary, and not regarded as a part of the system of foreign politics,

Thus by the Anglo-Saxon communities the world over is this magnificent experiment of self-government through representative assemblies being tried. Nowhere has any one system been devised and applied which is faultless; which evenly balances the legislative, executive, and judicial functions of government; which provides checks against hasty legislation without unduly embarrassing it; which secures the rights of minorities as well as of majorities; which gives free vent to legitimate discussion within and without the legislative halls, while throttling obstructive debate and preventing licentious criticisms; which distributes the control over domestic affairs to central and sectional assemblies, so as to

come to be studied by the intelligent Oriental, will he not see in them even more clearly than we have done a divine message, and interpret it for us more truly than we have tried to interpret it to him? At present his prejudices are aroused against it because it is the religion of the West, and the presentation of it by bigoted and often ignorant advocates of warring sects repels him from giving it independent and candid study. But as his political education grows and he comes to recognize the value of Western political institutions and apply them, will he not regard very differently that religion from which we have drawn our political inspiration, and see in it higher and deeper truths than we have yet elicited?

give the latter sufficient power without dangerously weakening the supremacy of cohesion which must reside in the central power; which has successfully defined the limits of State interference over industrial enterprise and State ownership of the media of commerce; which secures the independence of the judiciary both from executive influences, and from popular favor; which has defined a system of taxation that bears on the rich and the poor in proportion to their ability to support the weight; which, in fine, has created the perfect state, wherein no injustice and no inequality shall exist that it is possible for human interference to remove.

Is it not the mission of the English-speaking people, all the world over, to achieve this glorious consummation by the application of those same principles of liberty, which they have already embodied in so many more or less successful constitutions, and will this not be best done by effort and experiment along different lines rather than in one direction, and by many communities rather than by one?

CHAPTER VIII.

ANNEXATION FROM AMERICAN AND CANADIAN POINTS OF VIEW.

WHETHER the question be looked at from the point of view of an American or a Canadian, most impartial minds will come to one conclusion, that it would be better for the two great communities which divide the continent to live in closest commercial and social intercourse, but in separate houses. Canada has her own domestic troubles, and the United States has hers. To take typical examples:

The most perplexing problem that demands solution in Canada is the reconciliation of the English and the French races, involving Protestant and Catholic antagonism. This trouble would probably be most summarily settled by annexation, but if I were a citizen of the United States, I would consider it as a serious bar to that step.

The harmonizing of local interests over so vast an area as this country covers, is already a threatening trouble. It would not be rendered more easy by doubling its size. The divergent interests and habits of the North and South culminated in the Civil War. There is no such antagonism apparent to-day between any two sections of the Union, nor does there exist any local institution so dear to its friends and so abhorrent to its enemies as slavery. Nevertheless, the acrimony with which the silver question was discussed in the Senate, coupled with distinct geographical lines which separated the constituents which favored the remonetization of the white metal, and those which opposed it, is only one of many signs pointing to future complications, which it will require forbearance on the part of the electorate, and statesmanship of a high order on the part of the people's leaders, to solve without collisions.

Did Canada possess resources necessary to the development of the industrial interests of the United States, it might be desirable to negotiate for its absorption, but except ice, which Canada can ship in greater abundance and of superior quality to any made south of its line, Canada would simply swell the bulk of the same articles produced in excess by the Republic. Such being the case, would it not be wiser on the part of the United States to leave Canada to settle her own political and religious accounts, rather than to assume them and thus add other sectional issues and local interests to the many which already embarrass legislation in this country?

The homogeneity of the French Canadian Catholic party will not be destroyed by annexation. Insignificant as the French population of Louisiana and the lower Mississippi was three quarters of a century has not sufficed to absorb it into the body politic. The French market-woman of New Orleans still dresses as a Frenchwoman, speaks French, and thinks French, as unequivocally as her sister who drives her little cart filled with vegetables and flowers from the Beauport flats into the Quebec market on a Saturday morning.

Add one and a half millions of French to

the same number already in the States, and bring these three millions into antagonism with the other sixty-three millions of the United States, and the three millions would become an even more concrete unit than they are to-day. It would organize and stand unflinchingly on the defensive to preserve its religious, social, and judicial institutions. Its solid vote would at once become an object of bargain and sale in the American political market.

The Roman Catholic Church in the United States, already divided into Liberal and Conservative wings, feels the impossibility of resisting the impulse of American ideas, especially on the subject of education and common schools, and the liberal prelates, having enlisted the Papal Delegate and the Pope on their side, have advocated and in places carried into practice a nondescript combination of secular and ecclesiastical education, which must be an abomination to Cardinal Taschereau and the whole ultramontane Church of Canada. There is as wide a gap between the practical catholicism of Cardinal Gibbons and that of Cardinal Taschereau as between an extreme radical and an extreme conservative. The radical and the conservative in politics agree on the fundamental principles of representative government; but differ not only as to their scope but also as to the method of applying them. The two Cardinals are orthodox Catholics, so far as orthodoxy consists in assenting to certain theoretical theological dogmas, but the Baltimore churchman is imbued with the spirit of the nineteenth century, while the Quebec churchman is the lineal descendant of Bishop Laval, and the spiritual inheritor of the traditions of the Middle Ages. The American Cardinal believes the Church can only lead the age by keeping in touch with it; the Canadian Cardinal believes the age is rotten to the core, and the Church must raise it—not lead it. The American prelate knows that it is impossible to arrest the progress of secular education in his great flock; the Canadian believes the temporal and eternal salvation of every human soul is best secured by ignorance of the world, its evil ways, and pernicious profane literature. The one professes to see in the social and political impulses of the age, and especially in this country, forces elevating the race to a higher standard of true liberty; the other can see in them only the motives of irreligious license. The one approves of even secret societies whose objects are philanthropical, or are organized to give effect to labor combinations. The other anathematizes all who take an oath which imposes secrecy between the individual and his confessor. Both are Catholics, both may be orthodox, but the influence on the political opinions of the millions of subject souls which is exerted by the American Cardinal-Archbishop is widely different from that which the Canadian Cardinal-Archbishop would exert, if they changed Sees. Nor is the wide divergence of views and teaching a matter of merely individual variation. Each prelate but reflects the prevalent temper and policy of the large section of the Church over which he presides. Other subjects in this country may overshadow in political importance, the claims of the Church to dictate to its adherents, not only what they are to believe, but what they are to do; but few subjects can in reality be of more vital moment. Therefore, if there are degrees of intolerance within the Church, it is the part of every good citizen to strengthen its liberal wing by resisting the accession to the ultramontane party of such an overwhelming force, as would be the addition in bulk of French Canadian Catholicism. Roman Catholic liberals should be even more anxious than Protestants, to prevent so heavy a mass of unyielding intolerance being dropped into the scale, already loaded with sufficient home bigotry. The Roman Catholic Church is the most magnificently organized institution on earth. With unbending rigidity of dogma, it has at times exhibited flexibility in accommodating itself to special social and political conditions. It would not be the power it is to-day had it not done so. Were its incalculably great forces directed towards the same object which every true lover of his country has at heart, no one should seriously object if the methods employed are not altogether in harmony with his own, provided the end to be attained is the same. Although from the very nature of its claim and pretentions the Church is illiberal, there is a certain section of its clergy in this country which aims at bringing it into closer harmony with modern ideas and aspirations. The efforts of that section should be strengthened. They would be crushed under the dead weight of Canadian Catholicism.

On the other hand, looking at the question from a Canadian point of view, the dense population of sections of the United States, the prodigious development of corporative industrial enterprises, and the dangerous growth of individual wealth, have in the United States produced an acute phase of the labor problem from which Canada is practically free, and in which Canada, if wise, will hesitate to embroil herself.

The problems of life, industrial and social, are much more complicated south than north of the line. The physical advantages of the United States have been the chief cause of its inordinately rapid growth in prosperity. As a consequence the rapid accumulation of wealth by corporations and individuals is exciting not only an acute phase of the labor question, but is raising social barriers between the rich and the less rich ; is cutting up society into cliques and classes, whose distinguishing badge is the possession of so many millions more or less, and has already created an aristocracy of wealth which has unwritten laws, habits, and modes of speech of its own, as distinct as those which separate the nobility from the commonalty in the old world. This evil is the inevitable result of the accumulation of wealth, and will bring with it as inevitably its own retribution. The Canadian rich man, like the American rich man, wants to get out of his money all that money can give, not only of luxury but class distinction. Fortunately for Canada and the Canadians, it and they must grow rich more slowly, and some of the evils which accompany rapid inflation may be corrected as they arise, and before they expand to such dangerous proportions as they have already assumed in the **Great Republic**.

Poverty, a severe climate, land which can only be cleared and cultivated by labor, and mineral wealth which must be looked for and then won slowly by hard toil, are not unmixed evils, and should generate a race of hardy fibre, which may be happier if not richer than their neighbors born in a more hospitable clime.

If Canada, as a country, is really not to gain much if anything, industrially, by annexation, why should she submit to the shock of the operation which such a radical political change undoubtedly would produce? What she and the United States would gain by annexation, can be secured by reciprocal trade relations which, if not found to be advantageous, can be modified with much less friction than uncongenial political ties can be severed. This, however, Canada should recollect, that she is a body politic of 5,000,000 inhabitants, side by side with 63,000,000, and that if she is to remain at peace and harmony with her neighbor she must, as far as is consistent with self-respect and independence, shape her policy in conformity with her neighbor's, and strive to avoid needless causes of irritation. In the fishery controversy, in the canal controversy, and in the railroad controversy she has displayed a spirit of bumptiousness in her acts and utterances which, however well fitted to draw down party applause on party leaders, is not so well fitted to propitiate the good will of the 63,000,000 people.

In the great family of nations, as in the narrow circle of our home, we should "bear and forbear." In obedience to this rule arbitration is taking the place of war in the settlement of national disputes; and if Imperial Federation, and later a confederation of all the Anglo-Saxon communities, is ever effected, it will be only because the separate members waive supposed rights in deference to the general will and weal. Such a confederation may be to-day but a dream. It depends largely on Canada in her relations with the United States, whether it shall ever become a reality.

It is possible for Canada to remain independent, and yet prove to her neighbor that civility is not servility, and that independent units of the race may be more helpful to one another, and more stimulating to healthy political and commercial rivalry than if organically one. This fact once fully recognized, the practice as well as the principle of international aid and rivalry would expand and spread till it embraced all the English-speaking peoples of both hemispheres, and they would become a power on the earth irresistible, through moral strength more than even by numbers.

To achieve this it would not be necessary, as Mr. Carnegie conceives, that there should be uniformity of political institutions. There exists a unity of design in the constitutions of all the Anglo-Saxon communities, but a wide diversity of form. As in the animal and vegetable kingdoms we admire diversity in unity, and recognize the advantages and beauty which accrue from the prolific variations from original types, and as in society life would be unendurably monotonous, and progress in all directions slow, if human character did not combine infinite individuality with substantial uniformity, so in such a confederation of congenial but distinct States there might exist wide divergence of institutions, if only the same spirit and guiding principle animated all.

INDEX.

American colonies, relation to King and Parliament, 8
American colonies, relation to the mother country, 7
American colonies, trade restrictions, 21
Annexation and naturalization, 36
Annexation or independence, the immediate alternative, 11
Annexation, effect on mining, 69
Annexation, probable influence on Canadian material prosperity, 66
Annexation should be decided on by consideration of common good, 43
Annexation would impose on Canada the fiscal policy of the United States, 73
Annexation would increase sectional issues in the United States, 99
Annexation would not transfer established industries from their present centres, 66
Annexation would raise the provincial debts, 66
Annexation would strengthen English sympathy in the United States, 43
Australia, climate attracts immigrants, 51
Australia, debt a balance wheel, 3
Australia, freedom from external complications, 3
Australia, rapid growth of population, 48
Australia, tendency to communism, 50

Beef exports of the United States and Canada, 74
Behring Sea negotiations, 14
Butter exports of the United States and Canada, 76

Canada's attachment to the mother country, 9, 39
Canada's climate repels immigrants, 51
Canada's copper mines worked by foreigners, 72
Canada dependent for defence on Great Britain, 5

Index.

Canada's exports of agricultural products compared with those of the United States, 74
Canada's free lands less attractive than those of the United States, 57
Canada's physical disabilities, 63
Canada's production of iron and steel, 70
Canada should compete in the markets of the world, 79
Canada's slow growth in population compared with that of some other countries, 47
Canadian annexation or independence the alternative, 11, 34
Canadian conservatism opposed to commercial union, 8
Canadian lumber should be manufactured in Canada for foreign markets, 69
Canadian political relations, change inevitable with growth, 1
Canadian rebellion of 1837, 9
Cheese exports of the United States and Canada, 75
Climate determines the flow of immigration to sections of the United States, 51
Climate of Dakota is checking immigration, 58
Climate of Maine, its effect on immigration, 51
Commercial friction between Canada and the United States a source of danger, 4
Competition ultimately defeats protection, 21
Constitution of Canada compared with that of the United States, 84
Control of her foreign relations necessary to Canada, 13

Fishing industry of the Maritime Provinces would benefit by commercial union, 77
Free-trade policy of Great Britain, 21
French-Canadians a political unit, 100
French in Louisiana, 99

Gibbons, Cardinal, Catholic liberalism compared with Cardinal Taschereau's ultramontanism, 100

Home rule in England, 89
Home rule under States' government in the United States, 90
House of Lords, 85

Immigration, change in character of that to the United States, 62
Immigration into the United States since the Revolution, 40
Imperial federation, advantage to Canada, 33
Imperial federation, its constitution must differ from that of the United States, 15

Index.

Imperial federation must rest on racial sympathies, 19
Imperial federation only possible among independent states, 12, 18, 20
Independence of British colonies will be effected by constitutional methods, 13
India may evolve a special form of representative government, 94
Interdependence of the branches of the English race, 18
Iron imports into Canada, 71
Iron mining and manufacturing in Canada, 70

Manufacturing in Canada limited by its small population, 63
Maritime Provinces resented coercion, 12
Mineral exploration necessarily slow in Canada, 53
Mining attracts immigrants, 53
Mining would be stimulated by annexation, 69

" National Policy " in Canada, why it has been disappointing, 56
Naturalization not always sought by Englishmen, Why? 34
Naval parade in New York while Behring Sea Commission was sitting, 42
Nova Scotian coal mining will be benefited by commercial freedom, 69
Nova Scotian iron resources, 70
Nova Scotian Scotch and the Scotch of Ontario, 78

Political forbearance essential to international harmony, 107
Population, Australian colonies, 48
Population, Canada's slow growth in, 46
Population of prairie States declining, 58
Population of the United States at time of Revolution, 40
Population of the United States, decennial growth, 49
Pork exports of the United States and Canada, 75
Protection and high wages, 55
Protection in the United States, 22

Reciprocity as devised by Mr. Blaine to protect United States protection, 25
Reciprocity between the United States and Canada, 26, 32
Reciprocity, treaties of, by European powers, 26
Reciprocity, will it confer prosperity on Canada ? 56
Religious antagonism in Canada, 97
Representative government, indifference of English colonists to any special system, 93
Representative government, no system yet perfect, 95

Representative government, will be perfected by the communities of the Anglo-Saxon race working in different directions, 96
Roman Catholicism in the United States compared with Roman Catholicism in Canada, 100

Sectionalism and its growth in the United States, 98
Senate of the United States, 86
South Africa, future of, 4
South African Confederation, 92

Trade relations can be more easily modified than constitutional alliances, 106
Trusts organized to bridle competition, 28

United Empire loyalist spirit still strong in Canada, 38
United States, attachment to England, 43
United States, decennial growth in population, 51
United States, England's commercial rival, 30
United States, population at the time of the Revolution, 40
United States, universal use of English language in the, and its effects, 41

Wages and annexation, 79
Wages in Canada itself would probably not be affected by annexation, 79
Wages, no United States standard of, 79
Wealth, its rapid growth and its effects on social life in the United States, 105
Wheat exports of the United States and Canada, 74

Zollverein, a measure of commercial self-defence by Great Britain, 30
Zollverein proposed by Lord Salisbury, 21

www.ingramcontent.com/pod-product-compliance
Lightning Source LLC
Chambersburg PA
CBHW020124170426
43199CB00009B/622